THE POEMS OF

RUDYARD KIPLING

Table of Contents

A Pilgrim's Way 1
An Almanac of Twelve Sports 3
Belts 7
Bill 'Awkins 9
Cells 10
Cholera Camp 12
Cities And Thrones And Powers 14
Danny Deever 15
Dedication 17
Edgehill Fight 19
For to Admire 21
Fuzzy-wuzzy 23
Gentleman-Rankers 25
Gunga Din 27
If-- 30
Loot 32
Mandalay 35
My Boy Jack 37
Oonts 38
Recessional 40
Screw-guns 42
Shillin' a Day 44
Six Honest Serving Men 45
'Snarleyow' 46
Soldier, Soldier 48
The Answer 50
The Ballad Of East And West 51
The 'Eathen 55
The Explanation 58
The Female Of The Species 59

The Gods Of The Copybook Headings ... 61
The Legend Of Evil ... 64
The Lost Legion ... 67
The Miracles ... 70
The Power Of The Dog ... 72
The Shut-Eye Sentry ... 74
The Song Of The Dead ... 77
The Sons Of Martha ... 80
The Vampire ... 82
The White Man's Burden ... 84
The Widow at Windsor ... 86
The Young British Soldier ... 88
To Wolcott Balestier ... 91
Tommy ... 93
When Earth's Last Picture Is Painted ... 95

A Pilgrim's Way

I do not look for holy saints to guide me on my way,
Or male and female devilkins to lead my feet astray.
If these are added, I rejoice---if not, I shall not mind,
So long as I have leave and choice to meet my fellow-kind.
For as we come and as we go (and deadly-soon go we!)
The people, Lord, Thy people, are good enough for me!

Thus I will honour pious men whose virtue shines so bright
(Though none are more amazed than I when I by chance do right),
And I will pity foolish men for woe their sins have bred
(Though ninety-nine per cent. of mine I brought on my own head).
And, Amorite or Eremite, or General Averagee,
The people, Lord, Thy people, are good enough for me!

And when they bore me overmuch, I will not shake mine ears,
Recalling many thousand such whom I have bored to tears.
And when they labour to impress, I will not doubt nor scoff;
Since I myself have done no less and---sometimes pulled it off.
Yea, as we are and we are not, and we pretend to be,
The people, Lord, Thy people, are good enough for me!

And when they work me random wrong, as oftentimes hath been,
I will not cherish hate too long (my hands are none too clean).
And when they do me random good I will not feign surprise.
No more than those whom I have cheered with wayside charities.
But, as we give and as we take---whate'er our takings be---
The people, Lord, Thy people, are good enough for me!

But when I meet with frantic folk who sinfully declare
There is no pardon for their sin, the same I will not spare
Till I have proved that Heaven and Hell which in our hearts we have
Show nothing irredeemable on either side of the grave.

For as we live and as we die---if utter Death there be---
The people, Lord, Thy people, are good enough for me!

Deliver me from every pride---the Middle, High, and Low---
That bars me from a brother's side, whatever pride he show.
And purge me from all heresies of thought and speech and pen
That bid me judge him otherwise than I am judged. Amen!
That I may sing of Crowd or King or road-borne company,
That I may labour in my day, vocation and degree,
To prove the same in deed and name, and hold unshakenly
(Where'er I go, whate'er I know, whoe'er my neighbor be)
This single faith in Life and Death and to Eternity:
``The people, Lord, Thy people, are good enough for me!"

An Almanac of Twelve Sports

Here is a horse to tame--
    Here is a gun to handle--
    God knows you can enter the game
    If you'll only pay for the same,
      And the price of the game is a candle--
        One single flickering candle!

Hunting - January

    Certes it is a noble sport
      And men have quitted selle and swum for't,
    But I am of a meeker sort
      And I prefer Surtees in comfort.

    Reach down my "Handley Cross" again.
      My run, where never danger lurks, is
    With Jorrocks and his deathless train
      Pigg, Binjimin and Arterxerxes!

Coursing - February

    Most men harry the world for fun--
      Each man seeks it a different way
    But "of all daft devils under the sun
      A grey'ound's the daftest" said Jorrocks J.

Racing - March

    The horse is ridden--the jockey rides--
      The backers back--the owners own
    But ... there are lots of things besides,
      And I should leave this play alone.

Boating - April

> The Pope of Rome he could not win
> From pleasant meat and pleasant sin
> These who, in honour's hope, endure
> Lean days and lives enforced pure.
> These who, replying not, submit
> Unto the curses of the Pit
> Which he that rides (O greater shame!)
> Flings forth by number not by name...
> Could Triple Crown or Jesuit's oath
> Do what yon shuffle-stocking doth?

Fishing - May

> Behold a parable! A fished for B.
> C took her bait; her heart was set on D.
> Thank Heaven, who cooled your blood and cramped your wishes,
> Men and not Gods torment you, little fishes.

Cricket - June

> Thank God who made the British Isles
>   And taught me how to play,
> I do not worship crocodiles
>   Or bow the knee to clay!
>
> Give me a willow wand and I,
>   With hide and cork and twine,
> From century to century
>   Will gambol round my Shrine.

Archery - July

> The child of the Nineties considers with laughter
> The maid whom his Sire in the sixties ran after,
> While careering himself in pursuit of a girl whom
> The Twenties will dub a "last century heir-loom."

Coaching - August

> The Pious Horse to church may trot.
>   A maid may work a man's salvation.
> Four horses and a girl are not,
>   However, aids to reformation.

Shooting - September

> "Peace upon Earth, Goodwill to men!"
>   So greet we Christmas Day.
> Oh Christian load your gun and then,
>   O Christian, out and slay!

Golf - October

> Why Golf is Art and Art is Golf
>   we have not far to seek--
> So much depends upon the lie,
>   so much upon the cleek.

Boxing - November

> Read here the Moral roundly writ
>   For him that into battle goes--
> Each soul that, hitting hard and hit,
>   Encounters gross or ghostly foes:--

Prince, blown by many overthrows
  Half blind with shame, half choked with dirt
Man cannot tell but Allah knows
  How much the other side was hurt!

Skating - December

  Over the ice she flies
    Perfect and poised and fair--
  Stars in my true-love's eyes
    Teach me to do and to dare!

  Now will I fly as she flies ...
    Woe for the stars that misled!
  Stars that I saw in her eyes
  Now do I see in my head!

  Now we must come away.
    What are you out of pocket?
  'Sorry to spoil your play,
  But Somebody says we must pay--
    And the candle's down to the socket--
      Its horrible tallowy socket!

Belts

There was a row in Silver Street that's near to Dublin Quay,
Between an Irish regiment an' English cavalree;
It started at Revelly an' it lasted on till dark:
The first man dropped at Harrison's, the last forninst the Park.
For it was: -- "Belts, belts, belts, an' that's one for you!"
An' it was "Belts, belts, belts, an' that's done for you!"
O buckle an' tongue
Was the song that we sung
From Harrison's down to the Park!

There was a row in Silver Street -- the regiments was out,
They called us "Delhi Rebels", an' we answered "Threes about!"
That drew them like a hornet's nest -- we met them good an' large,
The English at the double an' the Irish at the charge.
Then it was: -- "Belts . . .

There was a row in Silver Street -- an' I was in it too;
We passed the time o' day, an' then the belts went whirraru!
I misremember what occurred, but subsequint the storm
A Freeman's Journal Supplemint was all my uniform.
O it was: -- "Belts . . .

There was a row in Silver Street -- they sent the Polis there,
The English were too drunk to know, the Irish didn't care;
But when they grew impertinint we simultaneous rose,
Till half o' them was Liffey mud an' half was tatthered clo'es.
For it was: -- "Belts . . .

There was a row in Silver Street -- it might ha' raged till now,
But some one drew his side-arm clear, an' nobody knew how;
'Twas Hogan took the point an' dropped; we saw the red blood run:
An' so we all was murderers that started out in fun.

While it was: -- "Belts . . .

There was a row in Silver Street -- but that put down the shine,
Wid each man whisperin' to his next: "'Twas never work o' mine!"
We went away like beaten dogs, an' down the street we bore him,
The poor dumb corpse that couldn't tell the bhoys were sorry for him.
When it was: -- "Belts . . .

There was a row in Silver Street -- it isn't over yet,
For half of us are under guard wid punishments to get;
'Tis all a merricle to me as in the Clink I lie:
There was a row in Silver Street -- begod, I wonder why!
But it was: -- "Belts, belts, belts, an' that's one for you!"
An' it was "Belts, belts, belts, an' that's done for you!"
O buckle an' tongue
Was the song that we sung
From Harrison's down to the Park!

Bill 'Awkins

"'As anybody seen Bill 'Awkins?"
"Now 'ow in the devil would I know?"
"'E's taken my girl out walkin',
An' I've got to tell 'im so --
Gawd -- bless -- 'im!
I've got to tell 'im so."

"D'yer know what 'e's like, Bill 'Awkins?"
"Now what in the devil would I care?"
"'E's the livin', breathin' image of an organ-grinder's monkey,
With a pound of grease in 'is 'air --
Gawd -- bless -- 'im!
An' a pound o' grease in 'is 'air."

"An' s'pose you met Bill 'Awkins,
Now what in the devil 'ud ye do?"
"I'd open 'is cheek to 'is chin-strap buckle,
An' bung up 'is both eyes, too --
Gawd -- bless -- 'im!
An' bung up 'is both eyes, too!"

"Look 'ere, where 'e comes, Bill 'Awkins!
Now what in the devil will you say?"
"It isn't fit an' proper to be fightin' on a Sunday,
So I'll pass 'im the time o' day --
Gawd -- bless -- 'im!
I'll pass 'im the time o' day!"

Cells

I've a head like a concertina: I've a tongue like a button-stick:
I've a mouth like an old potato, and I'm more than a little sick,
But I've had my fun o' the Corp'ral's Guard: I've made the cinders fly,
And I'm here in the Clink for a thundering drink
and blacking the Corporal's eye.
With a second-hand overcoat under my head,
And a beautiful view of the yard,
O it's pack-drill for me and a fortnight's C.B.
For "drunk and resisting the Guard!"
Mad drunk and resisting the Guard --
'Strewth, but I socked it them hard!
So it's pack-drill for me and a fortnight's C.B.
For "drunk and resisting the Guard."

I started o' canteen porter, I finished o' canteen beer,
But a dose o' gin that a mate slipped in, it was that that brought me here.
'Twas that and an extry double Guard that rubbed my nose in the dirt;
But I fell away with the Corp'ral's stock
and the best of the Corp'ral's shirt.

I left my cap in a public-house, my boots in the public road,
And Lord knows where, and I don't care, my belt and my tunic goed;
They'll stop my pay, they'll cut away the stripes I used to wear,
But I left my mark on the Corp'ral's face, and I think he'll keep it there!

My wife she cries on the barrack-gate, my kid in the barrack-yard,
It ain't that I mind the Ord'ly room -- it's ~that~ that cuts so hard.
I'll take my oath before them both that I will sure abstain,
But as soon as I'm in with a mate and gin, I know I'll do it again!
With a second-hand overcoat under my head,
And a beautiful view of the yard,
Yes, it's pack-drill for me and a fortnight's C.B.

For "drunk and resisting the Guard!"
Mad drunk and resisting the Guard --
'Strewth, but I socked it them hard!
So it's pack-drill for me and a fortnight's C.B.
For "drunk and resisting the Guard."

Cholera Camp

We've got the cholerer in camp -- it's worse than forty fights;
We're dyin' in the wilderness the same as Isrulites;
It's before us, an' be'ind us, an' we cannot get away,
An' the doctor's just reported we've ten more to-day!

Oh, strike your camp an' go, the Bugle's callin',
The Rains are fallin' --
The dead are bushed an' stoned to keep 'em safe below;
The Band's a-doin' all she knows to cheer us;
The Chaplain's gone and prayed to Gawd to 'ear us --
To 'ear us --
O Lord, for it's a-killin' of us so!

Since August, when it started, it's been stickin' to our tail,
Though they've 'ad us out by marches an' they've 'ad us back by rail;
But it runs as fast as troop-trains, and we cannot get away;
An' the sick-list to the Colonel makes ten more to-day.

There ain't no fun in women nor there ain't no bite to drink;
It's much too wet for shootin', we can only march and think;
An' at evenin', down the nullahs, we can 'ear the jackals say,
"Get up, you rotten beggars, you've ten more to-day!"

'Twould make a monkey cough to see our way o' doin' things --
Lieutenants takin' companies an' captains takin' wings,
An' Lances actin' Sergeants -- eight file to obey --
For we've lots o' quick promotion on ten deaths a day!

Our Colonel's white an' twitterly -- 'e gets no sleep nor food,
But mucks about in 'orspital where nothing does no good.
'E sends us 'eaps o' comforts, all bought from 'is pay --
But there aren't much comfort 'andy on ten deaths a day.

* * *

Our Chaplain's got a banjo, an' a skinny mule 'e rides,
An' the stuff 'e says an' sings us, Lord, it makes us split our sides!
With 'is black coat-tails a-bobbin' to Ta-ra-ra Boom-der-ay!
'E's the proper kind o' padre for ten deaths a day.

An' Father Victor 'elps 'im with our Roman Catholicks --
He knows an 'eap of Irish songs an' rummy conjurin' tricks;
An' the two they works together when it comes to play or pray;
So we keep the ball a-rollin' on ten deaths a day.

We've got the cholerer in camp -- we've got it 'ot an' sweet;
It ain't no Christmas dinner, but it's 'elped an' we must eat.
We've gone beyond the funkin', 'cause we've found it doesn't pay,
An' we're rockin' round the Distrck on ten deaths a day!

Then strike your camp an' go, the Rains are fallin',
The Bugle's callin'!
The dead are bushed an' stoned to keep 'em safe below!
An' them that do not like it they can lump it,
An' them that cannot stand it they can jump it;
We've got to die somewhere -- some way -- some'ow --
We might as well begin to do it now!
Then, Number One, let down the tent-pole slow,
Knock out the pegs an' 'old the corners -- so!
Fold in the flies, furl up the ropes, an' stow!
Oh, strike -- oh, strike your camp an' go!
(Gawd 'elp us!)

Cities And Thrones And Powers

Cities and Thrones and Powers,
Stand in Time's eye,
Almost as long as flowers,
Which daily die:
But, as new buds put forth,
To glad new men,
Out of the spent and unconsidered Earth, The Cities rise again.

This season's Daffodil,
She never hears
What change, what chance, what chill,
Cut down last year's:
But with bold countenance,
And knowledge small,
Esteems her seven days' continuance
To be perpetual.

So time that is o'er kind,
To all that be,
Ordains us e'en as blind,
As bold as she:
That in our very death,
And burial sure,
Shadow to shadow, well-persuaded, saith, "See how our works endure!"

Danny Deever

"What are the bugles blowin' for?" said Files-on-Parade.
"To turn you out, to turn you out", the Colour-Sergeant said.
"What makes you look so white, so white?" said Files-on-Parade.
"I'm dreadin' what I've got to watch", the Colour-Sergeant said.
For they're hangin' Danny Deever, you can hear the Dead March play,
The regiment's in 'ollow square -- they're hangin' him to-day;
They've taken of his buttons off an' cut his stripes away,
An' they're hangin' Danny Deever in the mornin'.

"What makes the rear-rank breathe so 'ard?" said Files-on-Parade.
"It's bitter cold, it's bitter cold", the Colour-Sergeant said.
"What makes that front-rank man fall down?" said Files-on-Parade.
"A touch o' sun, a touch o' sun", the Colour-Sergeant said.
They are hangin' Danny Deever, they are marchin' of 'im round,
They 'ave 'alted Danny Deever by 'is coffin on the ground;
An' 'e'll swing in 'arf a minute for a sneakin' shootin' hound --
O they're hangin' Danny Deever in the mornin'!

"'Is cot was right-'and cot to mine", said Files-on-Parade.
"'E's sleepin' out an' far to-night", the Colour-Sergeant said.
"I've drunk 'is beer a score o' times", said Files-on-Parade.
"'E's drinkin' bitter beer alone", the Colour-Sergeant said.
They are hangin' Danny Deever, you must mark 'im to 'is place,
For 'e shot a comrade sleepin' -- you must look 'im in the face;
Nine 'undred of 'is county an' the regiment's disgrace,
While they're hangin' Danny Deever in the mornin'.

"What's that so black agin' the sun?" said Files-on-Parade.
"It's Danny fightin' 'ard for life", the Colour-Sergeant said.
"What's that that whimpers over'ead?" said Files-on-Parade.
"It's Danny's soul that's passin' now", the Colour-Sergeant said.
For they're done with Danny Deever, you can 'ear the quickstep play,

The regiment's in column, an' they're marchin' us away;
Ho! the young recruits are shakin', an' they'll want their beer to-day,
After hangin' Danny Deever in the mornin'.

Dedication

To the City of Bombay

The Cities are full of pride,
Challenging each to each --
This from her mountain-side,
That from her burthened beach.

They count their ships full tale --
Their corn and oil and wine,
Derrick and loom and bale,
And rampart's gun-flecked line;
City by City they hail:
"Hast aught to match with mine?"

And the men that breed from them
They traffic up and down,
But cling to their cities' hem
As a child to their mother's gown.

When they talk with the stranger bands,
Dazed and newly alone;
When they walk in the stranger lands,
By roaring streets unknown;
Blessing her where she stands
For strength above their own.

(On high to hold her fame
That stands all fame beyond,
By oath to back the same,
Most faithful-foolish-fond;
Making her mere-breathed name
Their bond upon their bond.)

* * *

So thank I God my birth
Fell not in isles aside --
Waste headlands of the earth,
Or warring tribes untried --
But that she lent me worth
And gave me right to pride.

Surely in toil or fray
Under an alien sky,
Comfort it is to say:
"Of no mean city am I!"

(Neither by service nor fee
Come I to mine estate --
Mother of Cities to me,
For I was born in her gate,
Between the palms and the sea,
Where the world-end steamers wait.)

Now for this debt I owe,
And for her far-borne cheer
Must I make haste and go
With tribute to her pier.

And she shall touch and remit
After the use of kings
(Orderly, ancient, fit)
My deep-sea plunderings,
And purchase in all lands.
And this we do for a sign
Her power is over mine,
And mine I hold at her hands!

Edgehill Fight

Naked and gray the Cotswolds stand
Beneath the summer sun,
And the stubble fields on either hand
Where Sour and Avon run.
There is no change in the patient land
That has bred us every one.

She should have passed in cloud and fire
And saved us from this sin
Of war--red war--'twixt child and sire,
Household and kith and kin,
In the heart of a sleepy Midland shire,
With the harvest scarcely in.

But there is no change as we meet at last
On the brow-head or the plain,
And the raw astonished ranks stand fast
To slay or to be slain
By the men they knew in the kindly past
That shall never come again--

By the men they met at dance or chase,
In the tavern or the hall,
At the justice bench and the market place,
At the cudgel play or brawl--
Of their own blood and speech and race,
Comrades or neighbors all!

More bitter than death this day must prove
Whichever way it go,
For the brothers of the maids we love
Make ready to lay low

Their sisters' sweethearts, as we move
Against our dearest foe.

Thank Heaven! At last the trumpets peal
Before our strength gives way.
For King or for the Commonweal--
No matter which they say,
The first dry rattle of new-drawn steel
Changes the world today!

For to Admire

The Injian Ocean sets an' smiles
So sof', so bright, so bloomin' blue;
There aren't a wave for miles an' miles
Excep' the jiggle from the screw.
The ship is swep', the day is done,
The bugle's gone for smoke and play;
An' black agin' the settin' sun
The Lascar sings, "Hum deckty hai!"

For to admire an' for to see,
For to be'old this world so wide --
It never done no good to me,
But I can't drop it if I tried!

I see the sergeants pitchin' quoits,
I 'ear the women laugh an' talk,
I spy upon the quarter-deck
The orficers an' lydies walk.
I thinks about the things that was,
An' leans an' looks acrost the sea,
Till spite of all the crowded ship
There's no one lef' alive but me.

The things that was which I 'ave seen,
In barrick, camp, an' action too,
I tells them over by myself,
An' sometimes wonders if they're true;
For they was odd -- most awful odd --
But all the same now they are o'er,
There must be 'eaps o' plenty such,
An' if I wait I'll see some more.

* * *

Oh, I 'ave come upon the books,
An' frequent broke a barrick rule,
An' stood beside an' watched myself
Be'avin' like a bloomin' fool.
I paid my price for findin' out,
Nor never grutched the price I paid,
But sat in Clink without my boots,
Admirin' 'ow the world was made.

Be'old a crowd upon the beam,
An' 'umped above the sea appears
Old Aden, like a barrick-stove
That no one's lit for years an' years!
I passed by that when I began,
An' I go 'ome the road I came,
A time-expired soldier-man
With six years' service to 'is name.

My girl she said, "Oh, stay with me!"
My mother 'eld me to 'er breast.
They've never written none, an' so
They must 'ave gone with all the rest --
With all the rest which I 'ave seen
An' found an' known an' met along.
I cannot say the things I feel,
And so I sing my evenin' song:

For to admire an' for to see,
For to be'old this world so wide --
It never done no good to me,
But I can't drop it if I tried!

Fuzzy-wuzzy

(Soudan Expeditionary Force)

We've fought with many men acrost the seas,
An' some of 'em was brave an' some was not:
The Paythan an' the Zulu an' Burmese;
But the Fuzzy was the finest o' the lot.
We never got a ha'porth's change of 'im:
'E squatted in the scrub an' 'ocked our 'orses,
'E cut our sentries up at Sua~kim~,
An' 'e played the cat an' banjo with our forces.
So 'ere's ~to~ you, Fuzzy-Wuzzy, at your 'ome in the Soudan;
You're a pore benighted 'eathen but a first-class fightin' man;
We gives you your certificate, an' if you want it signed
We'll come an' 'ave a romp with you whenever you're inclined.

We took our chanst among the Khyber 'ills,
The Boers knocked us silly at a mile,
The Burman give us Irriwaddy chills,
An' a Zulu ~impi~ dished us up in style:
But all we ever got from such as they
Was pop to what the Fuzzy made us swaller;
We 'eld our bloomin' own, the papers say,
But man for man the Fuzzy knocked us 'oller.
Then 'ere's ~to~ you, Fuzzy-Wuzzy, an' the missis and the kid;
Our orders was to break you, an' of course we went an' did.
We sloshed you with Martinis, an' it wasn't 'ardly fair;
But for all the odds agin' you, Fuzzy-Wuz, you broke the square.

'E 'asn't got no papers of 'is own,
'E 'asn't got no medals nor rewards,
So we must certify the skill 'e's shown
In usin' of 'is long two-'anded swords:

When 'e's 'oppin' in an' out among the bush
With 'is coffin-'eaded shield an' shovel-spear,
An 'appy day with Fuzzy on the rush
Will last an 'ealthy Tommy for a year.
So 'ere's ~to~ you, Fuzzy-Wuzzy, an' your friends which are no more,
If we 'adn't lost some messmates we would 'elp you to deplore;
But give an' take's the gospel, an' we'll call the bargain fair,
For if you 'ave lost more than us, you crumpled up the square!

'E rushes at the smoke when we let drive,
An', before we know, 'e's 'ackin' at our 'ead;
'E's all 'ot sand an' ginger when alive,
An' 'e's generally shammin' when 'e's dead.
'E's a daisy, 'e's a ducky, 'e's a lamb!
'E's a injia-rubber idiot on the spree,
'E's the on'y thing that doesn't give a damn
For a Regiment o' British Infantree!
So 'ere's ~to~ you, Fuzzy-Wuzzy, at your 'ome in the Soudan;
You're a pore benighted 'eathen but a first-class fightin' man;
An' 'ere's ~to~ you, Fuzzy-Wuzzy, with your 'ayrick 'ead of 'air --
You big black boundin' beggar -- for you broke a British square!

Gentlemen-Rankers

To the legion of the lost ones, to the cohort of the damned,
To my brethren in their sorrow overseas,
Sings a gentleman of England cleanly bred, machinely crammed,
And a trooper of the Empress, if you please.
Yea, a trooper of the forces who has run his own six horses,
And faith he went the pace and went it blind,
And the world was more than kin while he held the ready tin,
But to-day the Sergeant's something less than kind.
We're poor little lambs who've lost our way,
Baa! Baa! Baa!
We're little black sheep who've gone astray,
Baa--aa--aa!
Gentlemen-rankers out on the spree,
Damned from here to Eternity,
God ha' mercy on such as we,
Baa! Yah! Bah!

Oh, it's sweet to sweat through stables, sweet to empty kitchen slops,
And it's sweet to hear the tales the troopers tell,
To dance with blowzy housemaids at the regimental hops
And thrash the cad who says you waltz too well.
Yes, it makes you cock-a-hoop to be "Rider" to your troop,
And branded with a blasted worsted spur,
When you envy, O how keenly, one poor Tommy being cleanly
Who blacks your boots and sometimes calls you "Sir".

If the home we never write to, and the oaths we never keep,
And all we know most distant and most dear,
Across the snoring barrack-room return to break our sleep,
Can you blame us if we soak ourselves in beer?
When the drunken comrade mutters and the great guard-lantern gutters
And the horror of our fall is written plain,

Every secret, self-revealing on the aching white-washed ceiling,
Do you wonder that we drug ourselves from pain?

We have done with Hope and Honour, we are lost to Love and Truth,
We are dropping down the ladder rung by rung,
And the measure of our torment is the measure of our youth.
God help us, for we knew the worst too young!
Our shame is clean repentance for the crime that brought the sentence,
Our pride it is to know no spur of pride,
And the Curse of Reuben holds us till an alien turf enfolds us
And we die, and none can tell Them where we died.
We're poor little lambs who've lost our way,
Baa! Baa! Baa!
We're little black sheep who've gone astray,
Baa--aa--aa!
Gentlemen-rankers out on the spree,
Damned from here to Eternity,
God ha' mercy on such as we,
Baa! Yah! Bah!

Gunga Din

You may talk o' gin and beer
When you're quartered safe out 'ere,
An' you're sent to penny-fights an' Aldershot it;
But when it comes to slaughter
You will do your work on water,
An' you'll lick the bloomin' boots of 'im that's got it.
Now in Injia's sunny clime,
Where I used to spend my time
A-servin' of 'Er Majesty the Queen,
Of all them blackfaced crew
The finest man I knew
Was our regimental bhisti, Gunga Din.
He was "Din! Din! Din!
You limpin' lump o' brick-dust, Gunga Din!
Hi! slippery ~hitherao~!
Water, get it! ~Panee lao~! [Bring water swiftly.]
You squidgy-nosed old idol, Gunga Din."

The uniform 'e wore
Was nothin' much before,
An' rather less than 'arf o' that be'ind,
For a piece o' twisty rag
An' a goatskin water-bag
Was all the field-equipment 'e could find.
When the sweatin' troop-train lay
In a sidin' through the day,
Where the 'eat would make your bloomin' eyebrows crawl,
We shouted "Harry By!" [Mr. Atkins's equivalent for "O brother."]
Till our throats were bricky-dry,
Then we wopped 'im 'cause 'e couldn't serve us all.
It was "Din! Din! Din!
You 'eathen, where the mischief 'ave you been?

You put some ~juldee~ in it [Be quick.]
Or I'll ~marrow~ you this minute [Hit you.]
If you don't fill up my helmet, Gunga Din!"

'E would dot an' carry one
Till the longest day was done;
An' 'e didn't seem to know the use o' fear.
If we charged or broke or cut,
You could bet your bloomin' nut,
'E'd be waitin' fifty paces right flank rear.
With 'is ~mussick~ on 'is back, [Water-skin.]
'E would skip with our attack,
An' watch us till the bugles made "Retire",
An' for all 'is dirty 'ide
'E was white, clear white, inside
When 'e went to tend the wounded under fire!
It was "Din! Din! Din!"
With the bullets kickin' dust-spots on the green.
When the cartridges ran out,
You could hear the front-files shout,
"Hi! ammunition-mules an' Gunga Din!"

I shan't forgit the night
When I dropped be'ind the fight
With a bullet where my belt-plate should 'a' been.
I was chokin' mad with thirst,
An' the man that spied me first
Was our good old grinnin', gruntin' Gunga Din.
'E lifted up my 'ead,
An' he plugged me where I bled,
An' 'e guv me 'arf-a-pint o' water-green:
It was crawlin' and it stunk,
But of all the drinks I've drunk,
I'm gratefullest to one from Gunga Din.

It was "Din! Din! Din!
'Ere's a beggar with a bullet through 'is spleen;
'E's chawin' up the ground,
An' 'e's kickin' all around:
For Gawd's sake git the water, Gunga Din!"

'E carried me away
To where a dooli lay,
An' a bullet come an' drilled the beggar clean.
'E put me safe inside,
An' just before 'e died,
"I 'ope you liked your drink", sez Gunga Din.
So I'll meet 'im later on
At the place where 'e is gone --
Where it's always double drill and no canteen;
'E'll be squattin' on the coals
Givin' drink to poor damned souls,
An' I'll get a swig in hell from Gunga Din!
Yes, Din! Din! Din!
You Lazarushian-leather Gunga Din!
Though I've belted you and flayed you,
By the livin' Gawd that made you,
You're a better man than I am, Gunga Din!

If—

If you can keep your head when all about you
Are losing theirs and blaming it on you;
If you can trust yourself when all men doubt you,
But make allowance for their doubting too;
If you can wait and not be tired by waiting,
Or, being lied about, don't deal in lies,
Or, being hated, don't give way to hating,
And yet don't look too good, nor talk too wise;

If you can dream - and not make dreams your master;
If you can think - and not make thoughts your aim;
If you can meet with triumph and disaster
And treat those two imposters just the same;
If you can bear to hear the truth you've spoken
Twisted by knaves to make a trap for fools,
Or watch the things you gave your life to broken,
And stoop and build 'em up with wornout tools;

If you can make one heap of all your winnings
And risk it on one turn of pitch-and-toss,
And lose, and start again at your beginnings
And never breath a word about your loss;
If you can force your heart and nerve and sinew
To serve your turn long after they are gone,
And so hold on when there is nothing in you
Except the Will which says to them: "Hold on";

If you can talk with crowds and keep your virtue,
Or walk with kings - nor lose the common touch;
If neither foes nor loving friends can hurt you;
If all men count with you, but none too much;
If you can fill the unforgiving minute

With sixty seconds' worth of distance run -
Yours is the Earth and everything that's in it,
And - which is more - you'll be a Man my son!

Loot

If you've ever stole a pheasant-egg be'ind the keeper's back,
If you've ever snigged the washin' from the line,
If you've ever crammed a gander in your bloomin' 'aversack,
You will understand this little song o' mine.
But the service rules are 'ard, an' from such we are debarred,
For the same with English morals does not suit.
(~Cornet~: Toot! toot!)
W'y, they call a man a robber if 'e stuffs 'is marchin' clobber
With the --
(~Chorus~) Loo! loo! Lulu! lulu! Loo! loo! Loot! loot! loot!
Ow the loot!
Bloomin' loot!
That's the thing to make the boys git up an' shoot!
It's the same with dogs an' men,
If you'd make 'em come again
Clap 'em forward with a Loo! loo! Lulu! Loot!
(~ff~) Whoopee! Tear 'im, puppy! Loo! loo! Lulu! Loot! loot! loot!

If you've knocked a nigger edgeways when 'e's thrustin' for your life,
You must leave 'im very careful where 'e fell;
An' may thank your stars an' gaiters if you didn't feel 'is knife
That you ain't told off to bury 'im as well.
Then the sweatin' Tommies wonder as they spade the beggars under
Why lootin' should be entered as a crime;
So if my song you'll 'ear, I will learn you plain an' clear
'Ow to pay yourself for fightin' overtime.
(~Chorus~) With the loot, . . .

Now remember when you're 'acking round a gilded Burma god
That 'is eyes is very often precious stones;
An' if you treat a nigger to a dose o' cleanin'-rod
'E's like to show you everything 'e owns.

When 'e won't prodooce no more, pour some water on the floor
Where you 'ear it answer 'ollow to the boot
(~Cornet~: Toot! toot!) --
When the ground begins to sink, shove your baynick down the chink,
An' you're sure to touch the --
(~Chorus~) Loo! loo! Lulu! Loot! loot! loot!
Ow the loot! . . .

When from 'ouse to 'ouse you're 'unting, you must always work in pairs --
It 'alves the gain, but safer you will find --
For a single man gets bottled on them twisty-wisty stairs,
An' a woman comes and clobs 'im from be'ind.
When you've turned 'em inside out, an' it seems beyond a doubt
As if there weren't enough to dust a flute
(~Cornet~: Toot! toot!) --
Before you sling your 'ook, at the 'ousetops take a look,
For it's underneath the tiles they 'ide the loot.
(~Chorus~) Ow the loot! . . .

You can mostly square a Sergint an' a Quartermaster too,
If you only take the proper way to go;
~I~ could never keep my pickin's, but I've learned you all I knew --
An' don't you never say I told you so.
An' now I'll bid good-bye, for I'm gettin' rather dry,
An' I see another tunin' up to toot
(~Cornet~: Toot! toot!) --
So 'ere's good-luck to those that wears the Widow's clo'es,
An' the Devil send 'em all they want o' loot!
(~Chorus~) Yes, the loot,
Bloomin' loot!
In the tunic an' the mess-tin an' the boot!
It's the same with dogs an' men,
If you'd make 'em come again

(~fff~) Whoop 'em forward with a Loo! loo! Lulu! Loot! loot! loot!
Heeya! Sick 'im, puppy! Loo! loo! Lulu! Loot! loot! loot!

Mandalay

By the old Moulmein Pagoda, lookin' eastward to the sea,
There's a Burma girl a-settin', and I know she thinks o' me;
For the wind is in the palm-trees, and the temple-bells they say:
"Come you back, you British soldier; come you back to Mandalay!"
Come you back to Mandalay,
Where the old Flotilla lay:
Can't you 'ear their paddles chunkin' from Rangoon to Mandalay?
On the road to Mandalay,
Where the flyin'-fishes play,
An' the dawn comes up like thunder outer China 'crost the Bay!

'Er petticoat was yaller an' 'er little cap was green,
An' 'er name was Supi-yaw-lat -- jes' the same as Theebaw's Queen,
An' I seed her first a-smokin' of a whackin' white cheroot,
An' a-wastin' Christian kisses on an 'eathen idol's foot:
Bloomin' idol made o'mud --
Wot they called the Great Gawd Budd --
Plucky lot she cared for idols when I kissed 'er where she stud!
On the road to Mandalay . . .

When the mist was on the rice-fields an' the sun was droppin' slow,
She'd git 'er little banjo an' she'd sing "Kulla-lo-lo!"
With 'er arm upon my shoulder an' 'er cheek agin' my cheek
We useter watch the steamers an' the hathis pilin' teak.
Elephints a-pilin' teak
In the sludgy, squdgy creek,
Where the silence 'ung that 'eavy you was 'arf afraid to speak!
On the road to Mandalay . . .

But that's all shove be'ind me -- long ago an' fur away,
An' there ain't no 'busses runnin' from the Bank to Mandalay;
An' I'm learnin' 'ere in London what the ten-year soldier tells:

"If you've 'eard the East a-callin', you won't never 'eed naught else."
No! you won't 'eed nothin' else
But them spicy garlic smells,
An' the sunshine an' the palm-trees an' the tinkly temple-bells;
On the road to Mandalay . . .

I am sick o' wastin' leather on these gritty pavin'-stones,
An' the blasted Henglish drizzle wakes the fever in my bones;
Tho' I walks with fifty 'ousemaids outer Chelsea to the Strand,
An' they talks a lot o' lovin', but wot do they understand?
Beefy face an' grubby 'and --
Law! wot do they understand?
I've a neater, sweeter maiden in a cleaner, greener land!
On the road to Mandalay . . .

Ship me somewheres east of Suez, where the best is like the worst,
Where there aren't no Ten Commandments an' a man can raise a thirst;
For the temple-bells are callin', an' it's there that I would be --
By the old Moulmein Pagoda, looking lazy at the sea;
On the road to Mandalay,
Where the old Flotilla lay,
With our sick beneath the awnings when we went to Mandalay!
On the road to Mandalay,
Where the flyin'-fishes play,
An' the dawn comes up like thunder outer China 'crost the Bay!

My Boy Jack

"Have you news of my boy Jack?"
Not this tide.
"When d'you think that he'll come back?"
Not with this wind blowing, and this tide.

"Has any one else had word of him?"
Not this tide.
For what is sunk will hardly swim,
Not with this wind blowing, and this tide.

"Oh, dear, what comfort can I find?"
None this tide,
Nor any tide,
Except he did not shame his kind --
Not even with that wind blowing, and that tide.

Then hold your head up all the more,
This tide,
And every tide;
Because he was the son you bore,
And gave to that wind blowing and that tide!

Oonts

(Northern India Transport Train)

Wot makes the soldier's 'eart to penk, wot makes 'im to perspire?
It isn't standin' up to charge nor lyin' down to fire;
But it's everlastin' waitin' on a everlastin' road
For the commissariat camel an' 'is commissariat load.
O the oont, O the oont, O the commissariat oont!
With 'is silly neck a-bobbin' like a basket full o' snakes;
We packs 'im like an idol, an' you ought to 'ear 'im grunt,
An' when we gets 'im loaded up 'is blessed girth-rope breaks.

Wot makes the rear-guard swear so 'ard when night is drorin' in,
An' every native follower is shiverin' for 'is skin?
It ain't the chanst o' being rushed by Paythans from the 'ills,
It's the commissariat camel puttin' on 'is bloomin' frills!
O the oont, O the oont, O the hairy scary oont!
A-trippin' over tent-ropes when we've got the night alarm!
We socks 'im with a stretcher-pole an' 'eads 'im off in front,
An' when we've saved 'is bloomin' life 'e chaws our bloomin' arm.

The 'orse 'e knows above a bit, the bullock's but a fool,
The elephant's a gentleman, the battery-mule's a mule;
But the commissariat cam-u-el, when all is said an' done,
'E's a devil an' a ostrich an' a orphan-child in one.
O the oont, O the oont, O the Gawd-forsaken oont!
The lumpy-'umpy 'ummin'-bird a-singin' where 'e lies,
'E's blocked the whole division from the rear-guard to the front,
An' when we get him up again -- the beggar goes an' dies!

'E'll gall an' chafe an' lame an' fight -- 'e smells most awful vile;
'E'll lose 'isself for ever if you let 'im stray a mile;
'E's game to graze the 'ole day long an' 'owl the 'ole night through,

An' when 'e comes to greasy ground 'e splits 'isself in two.
O the oont, O the oont, O the floppin', droppin' oont!
When 'is long legs give from under an' 'is meltin' eye is dim,
The tribes is up be'ind us, and the tribes is out in front --
It ain't no jam for Tommy, but it's kites an' crows for 'im.

So when the cruel march is done, an' when the roads is blind,
An' when we sees the camp in front an' 'ears the shots be'ind,
Ho! then we strips 'is saddle off, and all 'is woes is past:
'E thinks on us that used 'im so, and gets revenge at last.
O the oont, O the oont, O the floatin', bloatin' oont!
The late lamented camel in the water-cut 'e lies;
We keeps a mile be'ind 'im an' we keeps a mile in front,
But 'e gets into the drinkin'-casks, and then o' course we dies.

Recessional

God of our fathers, known of old—
Lord of our far-flung battle line—
Beneath whose awful hand we hold
Dominion over palm and pine—
Lord God of Hosts, be with us yet,
Lest we forget—lest we forget!

The tumult and the shouting dies—
The Captains and the Kings depart—
Still stands Thine ancient sacrifice,
An humble and a contrite heart.
Lord God of Hosts, be with us yet,
Lest we forget—lest we forget!

Far-called our navies melt away—
On dune and headland sinks the fire—
Lo, all our pomp of yesterday
Is one with Nineveh and Tyre!
Judge of the Nations, spare us yet,
Lest we forget—lest we forget!

If, drunk with sight of power, we loose
Wild tongues that have not Thee in awe—
Such boastings as the Gentiles use,
Or lesser breeds without the Law—
Lord God of Hosts, be with us yet,
Lest we forget—lest we forget!

For heathen heart that puts her trust
In reeking tube and iron shard—
All valiant dust that builds on dust,
And guarding calls not Thee to guard.

For frantic boast and foolish word,
Thy Mercy on Thy People, Lord!
Amen.

Screw-guns

Smokin' my pipe on the mountings, sniffin' the mornin' cool,
I walks in my old brown gaiters along o' my old brown mule,
With seventy gunners be'ind me, an' never a beggar forgets
It's only the pick of the Army
that handles the dear little pets -- 'Tss! 'Tss!
For you all love the screw-guns -- the screw-guns they all love you!
So when we call round with a few guns,
o' course you will know what to do -- hoo! hoo!
Jest send in your Chief an' surrender --
it's worse if you fights or you runs:
You can go where you please, you can skid up the trees,
but you don't get away from the guns!

They sends us along where the roads are, but mostly we goes where they ain't:
We'd climb up the side of a sign-board an' trust to the stick o' the paint:
We've chivied the Naga an' Looshai, we've give the Afreedeeman fits,
For we fancies ourselves at two thousand,
we guns that are built in two bits -- 'Tss! 'Tss!
For you all love the screw-guns . . .

If a man doesn't work, why, we drills 'im an' teaches 'im 'ow to behave;
If a beggar can't march, why, we kills 'im an' rattles 'im into 'is grave.
You've got to stand up to our business an' spring without snatchin' or fuss.
D'you say that you sweat with the field-guns?
By God, you must lather with us -- 'Tss! 'Tss!
For you all love the screw-guns . . .

The eagles is screamin' around us, the river's a-moanin' below,
We're clear o' the pine an' the oak-scrub,
we're out on the rocks an' the snow,

An' the wind is as thin as a whip-lash what carries away to the plains
The rattle an' stamp o' the lead-mules --
the jinglety-jink o' the chains -- 'Tss! 'Tss!
For you all love the screw-guns . . .

There's a wheel on the Horns o' the Mornin',
an' a wheel on the edge o' the Pit,
An' a drop into nothin' beneath you as straight as a beggar can spit:
With the sweat runnin' out o' your shirt-sleeves,
an' the sun off the snow in your face,
An' 'arf o' the men on the drag-ropes
to hold the old gun in 'er place -- 'Tss! 'Tss!
For you all love the screw-guns . . .

Smokin' my pipe on the mountings, sniffin' the mornin' cool,
I climbs in my old brown gaiters along o' my old brown mule.
The monkey can say what our road was --
the wild-goat 'e knows where we passed.
Stand easy, you long-eared old darlin's!
Out drag-ropes! With shrapnel! Hold fast -- 'Tss! 'Tss!
For you all love the screw-guns -- the screw-guns they all love you!
So when we take tea with a few guns,
o' course you will know what to do -- hoo! hoo!
Jest send in your Chief an' surrender --
it's worse if you fights or you runs:
You may hide in the caves, they'll be only your graves,
but you can't get away from the guns!

Shillin' a Day

My name is O'Kelly, I've heard the Revelly
From Birr to Bareilly, from Leeds to Lahore,
Hong-Kong and Peshawur,
Lucknow and Etawah,
And fifty-five more all endin' in "pore".
Black Death and his quickness, the depth and the thickness,
Of sorrow and sickness I've known on my way,
But I'm old and I'm nervis,
I'm cast from the Service,
And all I deserve is a shillin' a day.
(Chorus) Shillin' a day,
Bloomin' good pay --
Lucky to touch it, a shillin' a day!

Oh, it drives me half crazy to think of the days I
Went slap for the Ghazi, my sword at my side,
When we rode Hell-for-leather
Both squadrons together,
That didn't care whether we lived or we died.
But it's no use despairin', my wife must go charin'
An' me commissairin' the pay-bills to better,
So if me you be'old
In the wet and the cold,
By the Grand Metropold, won't you give me a letter?
(Full chorus) Give 'im a letter --
'Can't do no better,
Late Troop-Sergeant-Major an' -- runs with a letter!
Think what 'e's been,
Think what 'e's seen,
Think of his pension an' ----

Gawd save the Queen

Six Honest Serving Men

I Keep six honest serving-men:
  (They taught me all I knew)
Their names are What and Where and When
  And How and Why and Who.
I send them over land and sea,
  I send them east and west;
But after they have worked for me,
  I give them all a rest.

I let them rest from nine till five.
  For I am busy then,
As well as breakfast, lunch, and tea,
  For they are hungry men:
But different folk have different views:
  I know a person small--
She keeps ten million serving-men,
  Who get no rest at all!
She sends 'em abroad on her own affairs,
  From the second she opens her eyes--
One million Hows, two million Wheres,
  And seven million Whys!

'Snarleyow'

This 'appened in a battle to a batt'ry of the corps
Which is first among the women an' amazin' first in war;
An' what the bloomin' battle was I don't remember now,
But Two's off-lead 'e answered to the name o' Snarleyow.
Down in the Infantry, nobody cares;
Down in the Cavalry, Colonel 'e swears;
But down in the lead with the wheel at the flog
Turns the bold Bombardier to a little whipped dog!

They was movin' into action, they was needed very sore,
To learn a little schoolin' to a native army corps,
They 'ad nipped against an uphill, they was tuckin' down the brow,
When a tricky, trundlin' roundshot give the knock to Snarleyow.

They cut 'im loose an' left 'im -- 'e was almost tore in two --
But he tried to follow after as a well-trained 'orse should do;
'E went an' fouled the limber, an' the Driver's Brother squeals:
"Pull up, pull up for Snarleyow -- 'is head's between 'is 'eels!"

The Driver 'umped 'is shoulder, for the wheels was goin' round,
An' there ain't no "Stop, conductor!" when a batt'ry's changin' ground;
Sez 'e: "I broke the beggar in, an' very sad I feels,
But I couldn't pull up, not for you -- your 'ead between your 'eels!"

'E 'adn't 'ardly spoke the word, before a droppin' shell
A little right the batt'ry an' between the sections fell;
An' when the smoke 'ad cleared away, before the limber wheels,
There lay the Driver's Brother with 'is 'ead between 'is 'eels.

Then sez the Driver's Brother, an' 'is words was very plain,
"For Gawd's own sake get over me, an' put me out o' pain."
They saw 'is wounds was mortial, an' they judged that it was best,

So they took an' drove the limber straight across 'is back an' chest.

The Driver 'e give nothin' 'cept a little coughin' grunt,
But 'e swung 'is 'orses 'andsome when it came to "Action Front!"
An' if one wheel was juicy, you may lay your Monday head
'Twas juicier for the niggers when the case begun to spread.

The moril of this story, it is plainly to be seen:
You 'avn't got no families when servin' of the Queen --
You 'avn't got no brothers, fathers, sisters, wives, or sons --
If you want to win your battles take an' work your bloomin' guns!
Down in the Infantry, nobody cares;
Down in the Cavalry, Colonel 'e swears;
But down in the lead with the wheel at the flog
Turns the bold Bombardier to a little whipped dog!

Soldier, Soldier

"Soldier, soldier come from the wars,
Why don't you march with my true love?"
"We're fresh from off the ship an' 'e's maybe give the slip,
An' you'd best go look for a new love."
New love! True love!
Best go look for a new love,
The dead they cannot rise, an' you'd better dry your eyes,
An' you'd best go look for a new love.

"Soldier, soldier come from the wars,
What did you see o' my true love?"
"I seed 'im serve the Queen in a suit o' rifle-green,
An' you'd best go look for a new love."

"Soldier, soldier come from the wars,
Did ye see no more o' my true love?"
"I seed 'im runnin' by when the shots begun to fly --
But you'd best go look for a new love."

"Soldier, soldier come from the wars,
Did aught take 'arm to my true love?"
"I couldn't see the fight, for the smoke it lay so white --
An' you'd best go look for a new love."

"Soldier, soldier come from the wars,
I'll up an' tend to my true love!"
"'E's lying on the dead with a bullet through 'is 'ead,
An' you'd best go look for a new love."

"Soldier, soldier come from the wars,
I'll down an' die with my true love!"
"The pit we dug'll 'ide 'im an' the twenty men beside 'im --

An' you'd best go look for a new love."

"Soldier, soldier come from the wars,
Do you bring no sign from my true love?"
"I bring a lock of 'air that 'e allus used to wear,
An' you'd best go look for a new love."

"Soldier, soldier come from the wars,
O then I know it's true I've lost my true love!"
"An' I tell you truth again -- when you've lost the feel o' pain
You'd best take me for your true love."
True love! New love!
Best take 'im for a new love,
The dead they cannot rise, an' you'd better dry your eyes,
An' you'd best take 'im for your true love.

The Answer

A Rose, in tatters on the garden path,
Cried out to God and murmured 'gainst His Wrath,
Because a sudden wind at twilight's hush
Had snapped her stem alone of all the bush.
And God, Who hears both sun-dried dust and sun,
Had pity, whispering to that luckless one,
"Sister, in that thou sayest We did not well --
What voices heardst thou when thy petals fell?"
And the Rose answered, "In that evil hour
A voice said, `Father, wherefore falls the flower?
For lo, the very gossamers are still.'
And a voice answered, `Son, by Allah's will!'"

Then softly as a rain-mist on the sward,
Came to the Rose the Answer of the Lord:
"Sister, before We smote the dark in twain,
Ere yet the stars saw one another plain,
Time, Tide, and Space, We bound unto the task
That thou shouldst fall, and such an one should ask."
Whereat the withered flower, all content,
Died as they die whose days are innocent;
While he who questioned why the flower fell
Caught hold of God and saved his soul from Hell.

The Ballad Of East And West

Oh, East is East, and West is West, and never the twain shall meet,
Till Earth and Sky stand presently at God's great Judgment Seat;
But there is neither East nor West, Border, nor Breed, nor Birth,
When two strong men stand face to face,
tho' they come from the ends of the earth!

Kamal is out with twenty men to raise the Border-side,
And he has lifted the Colonel's mare that is the Colonel's pride:
He has lifted her out of the stable-door between the dawn and the day,
And turned the calkins upon her feet, and ridden her far away.
Then up and spoke the Colonel's son that led a troop of the Guides:
"Is there never a man of all my men can say where Kamal hides?"
Then up and spoke Mahommed Khan, the son of the Ressaldar:
"If ye know the track of the morning-mist, ye know where his pickets are.
At dusk he harries the Abazai -- at dawn he is into Bonair,
But he must go by Fort Bukloh to his own place to fare,
So if ye gallop to Fort Bukloh as fast as a bird can fly,
By the favour of God ye may cut him off ere he win to the Tongue of Jagai.
But if he be past the Tongue of Jagai, right swiftly turn ye then,
For the length and the breadth of that grisly plain is sown with Kamal's men.
There is rock to the left, and rock to the right, and low lean thorn between,
And ye may hear a breech-bolt snick where never a man is seen."
The Colonel's son has taken a horse, and a raw rough dun was he,
With the mouth of a bell and the heart of Hell
and the head of the gallows-tree.
The Colonel's son to the Fort has won, they bid him stay to eat --
Who rides at the tail of a Border thief, he sits not long at his meat.
He's up and away from Fort Bukloh as fast as he can fly,

Till he was aware of his father's mare in the gut of the Tongue of Jagai,
Till he was aware of his father's mare with Kamal upon her back,
And when he could spy the white of her eye, he made the pistol crack.
He has fired once, he has fired twice, but the whistling ball went wide.
"Ye shoot like a soldier," Kamal said. "Show now if ye can ride."
It's up and over the Tongue of Jagai, as blown dustdevils go,
The dun he fled like a stag of ten, but the mare like a barren doe.
The dun he leaned against the bit and slugged his head above,
But the red mare played with the snaffle-bars, as a maiden plays with a glove.
There was rock to the left and rock to the right, and low lean thorn between,
And thrice he heard a breech-bolt snick tho' never a man was seen.
They have ridden the low moon out of the sky, their hoofs drum up the dawn,
The dun he went like a wounded bull, but the mare like a new-roused fawn.
The dun he fell at a water-course -- in a woful heap fell he,
And Kamal has turned the red mare back, and pulled the rider free.
He has knocked the pistol out of his hand -- small room was there to strive,
"'Twas only by favour of mine," quoth he, "ye rode so long alive:
There was not a rock for twenty mile, there was not a clump of tree,
But covered a man of my own men with his rifle cocked on his knee.
If I had raised my bridle-hand, as I have held it low,
The little jackals that flee so fast were feasting all in a row:
If I had bowed my head on my breast, as I have held it high,
The kite that whistles above us now were gorged till she could not fly."
Lightly answered the Colonel's son: "Do good to bird and beast,
But count who come for the broken meats before thou makest a feast.
If there should follow a thousand swords to carry my bones away,
Belike the price of a jackal's meal were more than a thief could pay.
They will feed their horse on the standing crop,
their men on the garnered grain,

The thatch of the byres will serve their fires when all the cattle are slain.
But if thou thinkest the price be fair, -- thy brethren wait to sup,
The hound is kin to the jackal-spawn, -- howl, dog, and call them up!
And if thou thinkest the price be high, in steer and gear and stack,
Give me my father's mare again, and I'll fight my own way back!"
Kamal has gripped him by the hand and set him upon his feet.
"No talk shall be of dogs," said he, "when wolf and gray wolf meet.
May I eat dirt if thou hast hurt of me in deed or breath;
What dam of lances brought thee forth to jest at the dawn with Death?"
Lightly answered the Colonel's son: "I hold by the blood of my clan:
Take up the mare for my father's gift -- by God, she has carried a man!"
The red mare ran to the Colonel's son, and nuzzled against his breast;
"We be two strong men," said Kamal then, "but she loveth the younger best.
So she shall go with a lifter's dower, my turquoise-studded rein,
My broidered saddle and saddle-cloth, and silver stirrups twain."
The Colonel's son a pistol drew and held it muzzle-end,
"Ye have taken the one from a foe," said he;
"will ye take the mate from a friend?"
"A gift for a gift," said Kamal straight; "a limb for the risk of a limb.
Thy father has sent his son to me, I'll send my son to him!"
With that he whistled his only son, that dropped from a mountain-crest --
He trod the ling like a buck in spring, and he looked like a lance in rest.
"Now here is thy master," Kamal said, "who leads a troop of the Guides,
And thou must ride at his left side as shield on shoulder rides.
Till Death or I cut loose the tie, at camp and board and bed,
Thy life is his -- thy fate it is to guard him with thy head.
So, thou must eat the White Queen's meat, and all her foes are thine,
And thou must harry thy father's hold for the peace of the Border-line,
And thou must make a trooper tough and hack thy way to power --
Belike they will raise thee to Ressaldar when I am hanged in Peshawur."

* * *

They have looked each other between the eyes, and there they found no fault,
They have taken the Oath of the Brother-in-Blood on leavened bread and salt:
They have taken the Oath of the Brother-in-Blood on fire and fresh-cut sod,
On the hilt and the haft of the Khyber knife, and the Wondrous Names of God.
The Colonel's son he rides the mare and Kamal's boy the dun,
And two have come back to Fort Bukloh where there went forth but one.
And when they drew to the Quarter-Guard, full twenty swords flew clear --
There was not a man but carried his feud with the blood of the mountaineer.
"Ha' done! ha' done!" said the Colonel's son.
"Put up the steel at your sides!
Last night ye had struck at a Border thief --
to-night 'tis a man of the Guides!"

Oh, East is East, and West is West, and never the twain shall meet,
Till Earth and Sky stand presently at God's great Judgment Seat;
But there is neither East nor West, Border, nor Breed, nor Birth,
When two strong men stand face to face,
tho' they come from the ends of the earth!

The 'Eathen

The 'eathen in 'is blindness bows down to wood an' stone;
'E don't obey no orders unless they is 'is own;
'E keeps 'is side-arms awful: 'e leaves 'em all about,
An' then comes up the regiment an' pokes the 'eathen out.

All along o' dirtiness, all along o' mess,
All along o' doin' things rather-more-or-less,
All along of abby-nay, kul, an' hazar-ho,
Mind you keep your rifle an' yourself jus' so!
The young recruit is 'aughty -- 'e draf's from Gawd knows where;
They bid 'im show 'is stockin's an' lay 'is mattress square;
'E calls it bloomin' nonsense -- 'e doesn't know no more --
An' then up comes 'is Company an' kicks 'im round the floor!

The young recruit is 'ammered -- 'e takes it very 'ard;
'E 'angs 'is 'ead an' mutters -- 'e sulks about the yard;
'E talks o' "cruel tyrants" 'e'll swing for by-an'-by,
An' the others 'ears an' mocks 'im, an' the boy goes orf to cry.

The young recruit is silly -- 'e thinks o' suicide;
'E's lost 'is gutter-devil; 'e 'asn't got 'is pride;
But day by day they kicks 'im, which 'elps 'im on a bit,
Till 'e finds 'isself one mornin' with a full an' proper kit.

Gettin' clear o' dirtiness, gettin' done with mess,
Gettin' shut o' doin' things rather-more-or-less;
Not so fond of abby-nay, kul, nor hazar-ho,
Learns to keep 'is rifle an' 'isself jus' so!

The young recruit is 'appy -- 'e throws a chest to suit;
You see 'im grow mustaches; you 'ear 'im slap 'is boot;
'E learns to drop the "bloodies" from every word 'e slings,

An' 'e shows an 'ealthy brisket when 'e strips for bars an' rings.

The cruel-tyrant-sergeants they watch 'im 'arf a year;
They watch 'im with 'is comrades, they watch 'im with 'is beer;
They watch 'im with the women at the regimental dance,
And the cruel-tyrant-sergeants send 'is name along for "Lance".

An' now 'e's 'arf o' nothin', an' all a private yet,
'Is room they up an' rags 'im to see what they will get;
They rags 'im low an' cunnin', each dirty trick they can,
But 'e learns to sweat 'is temper an' 'e learns to sweat 'is man.

An', last, a Colour-Sergeant, as such to be obeyed,
'E schools 'is men at cricket, 'e tells 'em on parade;
They sees 'em quick an' 'andy, uncommon set an' smart,
An' so 'e talks to orficers which 'ave the Core at 'eart.

'E learns to do 'is watchin' without it showin' plain;
'E learns to save a dummy, an' shove 'im straight again;
'E learns to check a ranker that's buyin' leave to shirk;
An' 'e learns to make men like 'im so they'll learn to like their work.

An' when it comes to marchin' he'll see their socks are right,
An' when it comes to action 'e shows 'em 'ow to sight;
'E knows their ways of thinkin' and just what's in their mind;
'E knows when they are takin' on an' when they've fell be'ind.

'E knows each talkin' corpril that leads a squad astray;
'E feels 'is innards 'eavin', 'is bowels givin' way;
'E sees the blue-white faces all tryin' 'ard to grin,
An' 'e stands an' waits an' suffers till it's time to cap 'em in.

An' now the hugly bullets come peckin' through the dust,
An' no one wants to face 'em, but every beggar must;

So, like a man in irons which isn't glad to go,
They moves 'em off by companies uncommon stiff an' slow.

Of all 'is five years' schoolin' they don't remember much
Excep' the not retreatin', the step an' keepin' touch.
It looks like teachin' wasted when they duck an' spread an' 'op,
But if 'e 'adn't learned 'em they'd be all about the shop!

An' now it's "'Oo goes backward?" an' now it's "'Oo comes on?"
And now it's "Get the doolies," an' now the captain's gone;
An' now it's bloody murder, but all the while they 'ear
'Is voice, the same as barrick drill, a-shepherdin' the rear.

'E's just as sick as they are, 'is 'eart is like to split,
But 'e works 'em, works 'em, works 'em till he feels 'em take the bit;
The rest is 'oldin' steady till the watchful bugles play,
An' 'e lifts 'em, lifts 'em, lifts 'em through the charge that wins the day!

The 'eathen in 'is blindness bows down to wood an' stone;
'E don't obey no orders unless they is 'is own;
The 'eathen in 'is blindness must end where 'e began,
But the backbone of the Army is the non-commissioned man!

Keep away from dirtiness -- keep away from mess.
Don't get into doin' things rather-more-or-less!
Let's ha' done with abby-nay, kul, an' hazar-ho;
Mind you keep your rifle an' yourself jus' so!

The Explanation

Love and Death once ceased their strife
At the Tavern of Man's Life.
Called for wine, and threw -- alas! --
Each his quiver on the grass.
When the bout was o'er they found
Mingled arrows strewed the ground.
Hastily they gathered then
Each the loves and lives of men.
Ah, the fateful dawn deceived!
Mingled arrows each one sheaved;
Death's dread armoury was stored
With the shafts he most abhorred;
Love's light quiver groaned beneath
Venom-headed darts of Death.

Thus it was they wrought our woe
At the Tavern long ago.
Tell me, do our masters know,
Loosing blindly as they fly,
Old men love while young men die?

The Female Of The Species

When the Himalayan peasant meets the he-bear in his pride,
He shouts to scare the monster who will often turn aside.
But the she-bear thus accosted rends the peasant tooth and nail,
For the female of the species is more deadly than the male.

When Nag, the wayside cobra, hears the careless foot of man,
He will sometimes wriggle sideways and avoid it if he can,
But his mate makes no such motion where she camps beside the trail -
For the female of the species is more deadly than the male.

When the early Jesuit fathers preached to Hurons and Choctaws,
They prayed to be delivered from the vengeance of the squaws -
'Twas the women, not the warriors, turned those stark enthusiasts pale -
For the female of the species is more deadly than the male.

Man's timid heart is bursting with the things he must not say,
For the Woman that God gave him isn't his to give away;
But when hunter meets with husband, each confirms the others tale -
The female of the species is more deadly than the male.

Man, a bear in most relations, worm and savage otherwise,
Man propounds negotiations, Man accepts the compromise;
Very rarely will he squarely push the logic of a fact
To its ultimate conclusion in unmitigated act.

Fear, or foolishness, impels him, ere he lay the wicked low,
To concede some form of trial even to his fiercest foe.
Mirth obscene diverts his anger; Doubt and Pity oft perplex
Him in dealing with an issue - to the scandal of the Sex!

But the Woman that God gave him, every fibre of her frame
Proves her launched for one sole issue, armed and engined for the same,

And to serve that single issue, lest the generations fail,
The female of the species must be deadlier than the male.

She who faces Death by torture for each life beneath her breast
May not deal in doubt or pity - must not swerve for fact or jest.
These be purely male diversions - not in these her honor dwells -
She, the Other Law we live by, is that Law and nothing else!

She can bring no more to living than the powers that make her great
As the Mother of the Infant and the Mistress of the Mate;
And when Babe and Man are lacking and she strides unclaimed to claim
Her right as femme (and baron), her equipment is the same.

She is wedded to convictions - in default of grosser ties;
Her contentions are her children, Heaven help him, who denies!
He will meet no cool discussion, but the instant, white-hot wild
Wakened female of the species warring as for spouse and child.

Unprovoked and awful charges - even so the she-bear fights;
Speech that drips, corrodes and poisons - even so the cobra bites;
Scientific vivisection of one nerve till it is raw,
And the victim writhes with anguish - like the Jesuit with the squaw!

So it comes that Man, the coward, when he gathers to confer
With his fellow-braves in council, dare not leave a place for her
Where, at war with Life and Conscience, he uplifts his erring hands
To some God of abstract justice - which no woman understands.

And Man knows it! Knows, moreover, that the Woman that God gave him
Must command but may not govern; shall enthrall but not enslave him.
And She knows, because She warns him and Her instincts never fail,
That the female of Her species is more deadly than the male!

The Gods Of The Copybook Headings

As I pass through my incarnations in every age and race, I make my proper
prostrations to the Gods of the Market-Place.
Peering through reverent fingers I watch them flourish and fall,
And the Gods of the Copybook Headings, I notice, outlast them all.

We were living in trees when they met us. They showed us each in turn.
That Water would certainly wet us, as Fire would certainly burn:
But we found them lacking in Uplift, Vision and Breath of Mind,
So we left them to teach the Gorillas while we followed the March of Mankind.

We moved as the Spirit listed. They never altered their pace,
Being neither cloud nor wind-borne like the Gods of the Market-Place;
But they always caught up with our progress, and presently word would come
That a tribe had been wiped off its icefield, or the lights had gone out in Rome.

With the Hopes that our World is built on they were utterly out of touch.
They denied that the Moon was Stilton; they denied she was even Dutch.
They denied that Wishes were Horses; they denied that a Pig had Wings.
So we worshipped the Gods of the Market Who promised these beautiful things.

When the Cambrian measures were forming, They promised perpetual peace.
They swore, if we gave them our weapons, that the wars of the tribes would
cease.

But when we disarmed They sold us and delivered us bound to our foe,
And the Gods of the Copybook Headings said: "Stick to the Devil you know."

On the first Feminian Sandstones we were promised the Fuller Life
(Which started by loving our neighbour and ended by loving his wife)
Till our women had no more children and the men lost reason and faith,
And the Gods of the Copybook Heading said: "The Wages of Sin is Death."

In the Carboniferous Epoch we were promised abundance for all,
By robbing selected Peter to pay for collective Paul; But, though we had plenty of money, there was nothing our money could buy,
And the Gods of the Copybook Heading said: "If you don't work you die."

Then the Gods of the Market tumbled, and their smooth-tongued wizards
withdrew,
And the hearts of the meanest were humbled and began to believe it was true
That All is not God that Glitters, and Two and Two make Four-
And the Gods of the Copybook Headings limped up to explain it once more.

As it will be in the future, it was at the birth of Man- There are only four things certain since Social Progress began:-
That the Dog returns to his Vomit and the Sow returns to her Mire,

And the burnt Fool's bandaged finger goes wobbling back to the Fire;
And that after this is accomplished, and the brave new world begins

When all men are paid for existing and no man must pay for his sins,
As surely as Water will wet us, as surely as Fire will burn,

The Gods of the Copybook Headings with terror and slaughter return!

The Legend Of Evil

I

This is the sorrowful story
Told when the twilight fails
And the monkeys walk together
Holding their neighbours' tails: --

"Our fathers lived in the forest,
Foolish people were they,
They went down to the cornland
To teach the farmers to play.

"Our fathers frisked in the millet,
Our fathers skipped in the wheat,
Our fathers hung from the branches,
Our fathers danced in the street.

"Then came the terrible farmers,
Nothing of play they knew,
Only. . .they caught our fathers
And set them to labour too!

"Set them to work in the cornland
With ploughs and sickles and flails,
Put them in mud-walled prisons
And -- cut off their beautiful tails!

"Now, we can watch our fathers,
Sullen and bowed and old,
Stooping over the millet,
Sharing the silly mould,
* * *

"Driving a foolish furrow,
Mending a muddy yoke,
Sleeping in mud-walled prisons,
Steeping their food in smoke.

"We may not speak to our fathers,
For if the farmers knew
They would come up to the forest
And set us to labour too."

This is the horrible story
Told as the twilight fails
And the monkeys walk together
Holding their kinsmen's tails.

II

'Twas when the rain fell steady an' the Ark was pitched an' ready,
That Noah got his orders for to take the bastes below;
He dragged them all together by the horn an' hide an' feather,
An' all excipt the Donkey was agreeable to go.

Thin Noah spoke him fairly, thin talked to him sevarely,
An' thin he cursed him squarely to the glory av the Lord: --
"Divil take the ass that bred you, and the greater ass that fed you --
Divil go wid you, ye spalpeen!" an' the Donkey went aboard.

But the wind was always failin', an' 'twas most onaisy sailin',
An' the ladies in the cabin couldn't stand the stable air;
An' the bastes betwuxt the hatches, they tuk an' died in batches,
Till Noah said: -- "There's wan av us that hasn't paid his fare!"

For he heard a flusteration 'mid the bastes av all creation --

The trumpetin' av elephints an' bellowin' av whales;
An' he saw forninst the windy whin he wint to stop the shindy
The Divil wid a stable-fork bedivillin' their tails.

The Divil cursed outrageous, but Noah said umbrageous: --
"To what am I indebted for this tenant-right invasion?"
An' the Divil gave for answer: -- "Evict me if you can, sir,
For I came in wid the Donkey -- on Your Honour's invitation."

The Lost Legion

There's a Legion that never was 'listed,
That carries no colours or crest,
But, split in a thousand detachments,
Is breaking the road for the rest.
Our fathers they left us their blessing --
They taught us, and groomed us, and crammed;
But we've shaken the Clubs and the Messes
To go and find out and be damned
(Dear boys!),
To go and get shot and be damned.

So some of us chivy the slaver,
And some of us cherish the black,
And some of us hunt on the Oil Coast,
And some on -- the Wallaby track:
And some of us drift to Sarawak,
And some of us drift up The Fly,
And some share our tucker with tigers,
And some with the gentle Masai
(Dear boys!),
Take tea with the giddy Masai.

We've painted The Islands vermilion,
We've pearled on half-shares in the Bay,
We've shouted on seven-ounce nuggets,
We've starved on a Seedeeboy's pay;
We've laughed at the world as we found it --
Its women and cities and men --
From Sayyid Burgash in a tantrum
To the smoke-reddened eyes of Loben
(Dear boys!),
We've a little account with Loben.

* * *

The ends o' the Earth were our portion,
The ocean at large was our share.
There was never a skirmish to windward
But the Leaderless Legion was there:
Yes, somehow and somewhere and always
We were first when the trouble began,
From a lottery-row in Manila,
To an I.D.B. race on the Pan
(Dear boys!),
With the Mounted Police on the Pan.

We preach in advance of the Army,
We skirmish ahead of the Church,
With never a gunboat to help us
When we're scuppered and left in the lurch.
But we know as the cartridges finish,
And we're filed on our last little shelves,
That the Legion that never was 'listed
Will send us as good as ourselves
(Good men!),
Five hundred as good as ourselves.

Then a health (we must drink it in whispers)
To our wholly unauthorised horde --
To the line of our dusty foreloopers,
The Gentlemen Rovers abroad --
Yes, a health to ourselves ere we scatter,
For the steamer won't wait for the train,
And the Legion that never was 'listed
Goes back into quarters again!
'Regards!
Goes back under canvas again.
Hurrah!

The swag and the billy again.
Here's how!
The trail and the packhorse again.
Salue!
The trek and the laager again.

The Miracles

I sent a message to my dear --
A thousand leagues and more to Her --
The dumb sea-levels thrilled to hear,
And Lost Atlantis bore to Her.

Behind my message hard I came,
And nigh had found a grave for me;
But that I launched of steel and flame
Did war against the wave for me.

Uprose the deep, by gale on gale,
To bid me change my mind again --
He broke his teeth along my rail,
And, roaring, swung behind again.

I stayed the sun at noon to tell
My way across the waste of it;
I read the storm before it fell
And made the better haste of it.

Afar, I hailed the land at night --
The towers I built had heard of me --
And, ere my rocket reached its height,
Had flashed my Love the word of me.

Earth sold her chosen men of strength
(They lived and strove and died for me)
To drive my road a nation's length,
And toss the miles aside for me.

I snatched their toil to serve my needs --
Too slow their fleetest flew for me --

I tired twenty smoking steeds,
And bade them bait a new for me.

I sent the lightnings forth to see
Where hour by hour She waited me.
Among ten million one was She,
And surely all men hated me!

Dawn ran to meet me at my goal --
Ah, day no tongue shall tell again!
And little folk of little soul
Rose up to buy and sell again!

The Power Of The Dog

There is sorrow enough in the natural way
From men and women to fill our day;
And when we are certain of sorrow in store,
Why do we always arrange for more?
Brothers and Sisters, I bid you beware
Of giving your heart to a dog to tear.

Buy a pup and your money will buy
Love unflinching that cannot lie--
Perfect passion and worship fed
By a kick in the ribs or a pat on the head.
Nevertheless it is hardly fair
To risk your heart for a dog to tear.

When the fourteen years which Nature permits
Are closing in asthma, or tumour, or fits,
And the vet's unspoken prescription runs
To lethal chambers or loaded guns,
Then you will find--it's your own affair--
But...you've given your heart for a dog to tear.

When the body that lived at your single will,
With its whimper of welcome, is stilled (how still!);
When the spirit that answered your every mood
Is gone--wherever it goes--for good,
You will discover how much you care,
And will give your heart for the dog to tear.

We've sorrow enough in the natural way,
When it comes to burying Christian clay.
Our loves are not given, but only lent,
At compound interest of cent per cent.

Though it is not always the case, I believe,
That the longer we've kept 'em, the more do we grieve:
For, when debts are payable, right or wrong,
A short-time loan is as bad as a long--
So why in Heaven (before we are there)
Should we give our hearts to a dog to tear?

The Shut-Eye Sentry

Sez the Junior Orderly Sergeant
To the Senior Orderly Man:
"Our Orderly Orf'cer's hokee-mut,
You 'elp 'im all you can.
For the wine was old and the night is cold,
An' the best we may go wrong,
So, 'fore 'e gits to the sentry-box,
You pass the word along."

So it was "Rounds! What Rounds?" at two of a frosty night,
'E's 'oldin' on by the sergeant's sash, but, sentry, shut your eye.
An' it was "Pass! All's well!" Oh, ain't 'e drippin' tight!
'E'll need an affidavit pretty badly by-an'-by.

The moon was white on the barricks,
The road was white an' wide,
An' the Orderly Orf'cer took it all,
An' the ten-foot ditch beside.
An' the corporal pulled an' the sergeant pushed,
An' the three they danced along,
But I'd shut my eyes in the sentry-box,
So I didn't see nothin' wrong.

Though it was "Rounds! What Rounds?" O corporal, 'old 'im up!
'E's usin' 'is cap as it shouldn't be used, but, sentry, shut your eye.
An' it was "Pass! All's well!" Ho, shun the foamin' cup!
'E'll need, etc.

'Twas after four in the mornin';
We 'ad to stop the fun,
An' we sent 'im 'ome on a bullock-cart,
With 'is belt an' stock undone;

But we sluiced 'im down an' we washed 'im out,
An' a first-class job we made,
When we saved 'im, smart as a bombardier,
For six-o'clock parade.

It 'ad been "Rounds! What Rounds?" Oh, shove 'im straight again!
'E's usin' 'is sword for a bicycle, but, sentry, shut your eye.
An' it was "Pass! All's well!" 'E's called me "Darlin' Jane"!
'E'll need, etc.

The drill was long an' 'eavy,
The sky was 'ot an' blue,
An' 'is eye was wild an' 'is 'air was wet,
But 'is sergeant pulled 'im through.
Our men was good old trusties --
They'd done it on their 'ead;
But you ought to 'ave 'eard 'em markin' time
To 'ide the things 'e said!

For it was "Right flank -- wheel!" for "'Alt, an' stand at ease!"
An' "Left extend!" for "Centre close!" O marker, shut your eye!
An' it was, "'Ere, sir, 'ere! before the Colonel sees!"
So he needed affidavits pretty badly by-an'-by.

There was two-an'-thirty sergeants,
There was corp'rals forty-one,
There was just nine 'undred rank an' file
To swear to a touch o' sun.
There was me 'e'd kissed in the sentry-box,
As I 'ave not told in my song,
But I took my oath, which were Bible truth,
I 'adn't seen nothin' wrong.

There's them that's 'ot an' 'aughty,

There's them that's cold an' 'ard,
But there comes a night when the best gets tight,
And then turns out the Guard.
I've seen them 'ide their liquor
In every kind o' way,
But most depends on makin' friends
With Privit Thomas A.!

When it is "Rounds! What Rounds?" 'E's breathin' through 'is nose.
'E's reelin', rollin', roarin' tight, but, sentry, shut your eye.
An' it is "Pass! All's well!" An' that's the way it goes:
We'll 'elp 'im for 'is mother, an' 'e'll 'elp us by-an'-by!

The Song Of The Dead

Hear now the Song of the Dead -- in the North by the torn berg-edges --

They that look still to the Pole, asleep by their hide-stripped sledges.
Song of the Dead in the South -- in the sun by their skeleton horses,
Where the warrigal whimpers and bays through the dust
of the sear river-courses.

Song of the Dead in the East -- in the heat-rotted jungle hollows,
Where the dog-ape barks in the kloof --
in the brake of the buffalo-wallows.
Song of the Dead in the West --
in the Barrens, the waste that betrayed them,
Where the wolverene tumbles their packs
from the camp and the grave-mound they made them;
Hear now the Song of the Dead!

I

We were dreamers, dreaming greatly, in the man-stifled town;
We yearned beyond the sky-line where the strange roads go down.
Came the Whisper, came the Vision, came the Power with the Need,
Till the Soul that is not man's soul was lent us to lead.
As the deer breaks -- as the steer breaks -- from the herd where they graze,
In the faith of little children we went on our ways.
Then the wood failed -- then the food failed -- then the last water dried --

In the faith of little children we lay down and died.
On the sand-drift -- on the veldt-side -- in the fern-scrub we lay,
That our sons might follow after by the bones on the way.
Follow after -- follow after! We have watered the root,

And the bud has come to blossom that ripens for fruit!
Follow after -- we are waiting, by the trails that we lost,
For the sounds of many footsteps, for the tread of a host.
Follow after -- follow after -- for the harvest is sown:
By the bones about the wayside ye shall come to your own!

When Drake went down to the Horn
And England was crowned thereby,
'Twixt seas unsailed and shores unhailed
Our Lodge -- our Lodge was born
(And England was crowned thereby!)

Which never shall close again
By day nor yet by night,
While man shall take his life to stake
At risk of shoal or main
(By day nor yet by night).

But standeth even so
As now we witness here,
While men depart, of joyful heart,
Adventure for to know
(As now bear witness here!)

II

We have fed our sea for a thousand years
And she calls us, still unfed,
Though there's never a wave of all her waves
But marks our English dead:
We have strawed our best to the weed's unrest,
To the shark and the sheering gull.
If blood be the price of admiralty,

Lord God, we ha' paid in full!

There's never a flood goes shoreward now
But lifts a keel we manned;
There's never an ebb goes seaward now
But drops our dead on the sand --
But slinks our dead on the sands forlore,
From the Ducies to the Swin.
If blood be the price of admiralty,
If blood be the price of admiralty,
Lord God, we ha' paid it in!

We must feed our sea for a thousand years,
For that is our doom and pride,
As it was when they sailed with the ~Golden Hind~,
Or the wreck that struck last tide --
Or the wreck that lies on the spouting reef
Where the ghastly blue-lights flare.
If blood be the price of admiralty,
If blood be the price of admiralty,
If blood be the price of admiralty,
Lord God, we ha' bought it fair!

The Sons Of Martha

The Sons of Mary seldom bother, for they have inherited that good part;
But the Sons of Martha favour their Mother of the careful soul and the troubled heart.
And because she lost her temper once, and because she was rude to the Lord her Guest,
Her Sons must wait upon Mary's Sons, world without end, reprieve, or rest.

It is their care in all the ages to take the buffet and cushion the shock.
It is their care that the gear engages; it is their care that the switches lock.
It is their care that the wheels run truly; it is their care to embark and entrain,
Tally, transport, and deliver duly the Sons of Mary by land and main.

They say to mountains ``Be ye removèd.'' They say to the lesser floods ``Be dry.''
Under their rods are the rocks reprovèd---they are not afraid of that which is high.
Then do the hill-tops shake to the summit---then is the bed of the deep laid bare,
That the Sons of Mary may overcome it, pleasantly sleeping and unaware.

They finger Death at their gloves' end where they piece and repiece the living wires.
He rears against the gates they tend: they feed him hungry behind their fires.
Early at dawn, ere men see clear, they stumble into his terrible stall,
And hale him forth like a haltered steer, and goad and turn him till evenfall.

* * *

To these from birth is Belief forbidden; from these till death is Relief afar.
They are concerned with matters hidden---under the earthline their altars are---
The secret fountains to follow up, waters withdrawn to restore to the mouth,
And gather the floods as in a cup, and pour them again at a city's drouth.

They do not preach that their God will rouse them a little before the nuts work loose.
They do not preach that His Pity allows them to drop their job when they damn-well choose.
As in the thronged and the lighted ways, so in the dark and the desert they stand,
Wary and watchful all their days that their brethren's ways may be long in the land.

Raise ye the stone or cleave the wood to make a path more fair or flat;
Lo, it is black already with the blood some Son of Martha spilled for that!
Not as a ladder from earth to Heaven, not as a witness to any creed,
But simple service simply given to his own kind in their common need.

And the Sons of Mary smile and are blessèd---they know the Angels are on their side.
They know in them is the Grace confessèd, and for them are the Mercies multiplied.
They sit at the feet---they hear the Word---they see how truly the Promise runs.
They have cast their burden upon the Lord, and---the Lord He lays it on Martha's Sons!

The Vampire

A fool there was and he made his prayer
(Even as you or I!)
To a rag and a bone and a hank of hair,
(We called her the woman who did not care),
But the fool he called her his lady fair--
(Even as you or I!)

Oh, the years we waste and the tears we waste,
And the work of our head and hand
Belong to the woman who did not know
(And now we know that she never could know)
And did not understand!

A fool there was and his goods he spent,
(Even as you or I!)
Honour and faith and a sure intent
(And it wasn't the least what the lady meant),
But a fool must follow his natural bent
(Even as you or I!)

Oh, the toil we lost and the spoil we lost
And the excellent things we planned
Belong to the woman who didn't know why
(And now we know that she never knew why)
And did not understand!

The fool was stripped to his foolish hide,
(Even as you or I!)
Which she might have seen when she threw him aside--
(But it isn't on record the lady tried)
So some of him lived but the most of him died--
(Even as you or I!)

* * *

``And it isn't the shame and it isn't the blame
That stings like a white-hot brand--
It's coming to know that she never knew why
(Seeing, at last, she could never know why)
And never could understand!"

The White Man's Burden

Take up the White Man's burden--
Send forth the best ye breed--
Go, bind your sons to exile
To serve your captives' need;
To wait, in heavy harness,
On fluttered folk and wild--
Your new-caught sullen peoples,
Half devil and half child.

Take up the White Man's burden--
In patience to abide,
To veil the threat of terror
And check the show of pride;
By open speech and simple,
An hundred times made plain,
To seek another's profit
And work another's gain.

Take up the White Man's burden--
The savage wars of peace--
Fill full the mouth of Famine,
And bid the sickness cease;
And when your goal is nearest
(The end for others sought)
Watch sloth and heathen folly
Bring all your hope to nought.

Take up the White Man's burden--
No iron rule of kings,
But toil of serf and sweeper--
The tale of common things.
The ports ye shall not enter,

The roads ye shall not tread,
Go, make them with your living
And mark them with your dead.

Take up the White Man's burden,
And reap his old reward--
The blame of those ye better
The hate of those ye guard--
The cry of hosts ye humour
(Ah, slowly!) toward the light:--
"Why brought ye us from bondage,
Our loved Egyptian night?"

Take up the White Man's burden--
Ye dare not stoop to less--
Nor call too loud on Freedom
To cloak your weariness.
By all ye will or whisper,
By all ye leave or do,
The silent sullen peoples
Shall weigh your God and you.

Take up the White Man's burden!
Have done with childish days--
The lightly-proffered laurel,
The easy ungrudged praise:
Comes now, to search your manhood
Through all the thankless years,
Cold, edged with dear-bought wisdom,
The judgment of your peers.

The Widow at Windsor

'Ave you 'eard o' the Widow at Windsor
With a hairy gold crown on 'er 'ead?
She 'as ships on the foam -- she 'as millions at 'ome,
An' she pays us poor beggars in red.
 (Ow, poor beggars in red!)
There's 'er nick on the cavalry 'orses,
There's 'er mark on the medical stores --
An' 'er troopers you'll find with a fair wind be'ind
That takes us to various wars.
 (Poor beggars! -- barbarious wars!)
Then 'ere's to the Widow at Windsor,
An' 'ere's to the stores an' the guns,
The men an' the 'orses what makes up the forces
O' Missis Victorier's sons.
 (Poor beggars! Victorier's sons!)

Walk wide o' the Widow at Windsor,
For 'alf o' Creation she owns:
We 'ave bought 'er the same with the sword an' the flame,
An' we've salted it down with our bones.
 (Poor beggars! -- it's blue with our bones!)
Hands off o' the sons o' the Widow,
Hands off o' the goods in 'er shop,
For the Kings must come down an' the Emperors frown
When the Widow at Windsor says "Stop"!
 (Poor beggars! -- we're sent to say "Stop"!)
Then 'ere's to the Lodge o' the Widow,
From the Pole to the Tropics it runs --
To the Lodge that we tile with the rank an' the file,
An' open in form with the guns.
 (Poor beggars! -- it's always they guns!)

* * *

We 'ave 'eard o' the Widow at Windsor,
It's safest to let 'er alone:
For 'er sentries we stand by the sea an' the land
Wherever the bugles are blown.
(Poor beggars! -- an' don't we get blown!)
Take 'old o' the Wings o' the Mornin',
An' flop round the earth till you're dead;
But you won't get away from the tune that they play
To the bloomin' old rag over'ead.
(Poor beggars! -- it's 'ot over'ead!)
Then 'ere's to the sons o' the Widow,
Wherever, 'owever they roam.
'Ere's all they desire, an' if they require
A speedy return to their 'ome.
(Poor beggars! -- they'll never see 'ome!)

The Young British Soldier

When the 'arf-made recruity goes out to the East
'E acts like a babe an' 'e drinks like a beast,
An' 'e wonders because 'e is frequent deceased
Ere 'e's fit for to serve as a soldier.
Serve, serve, serve as a soldier,
Serve, serve, serve as a soldier,
Serve, serve, serve as a soldier,
So-oldier of the Queen!

Now all you recruities what's drafted to-day,
You shut up your rag-box an' 'ark to my lay,
An' I'll sing you a soldier as far as I may:
A soldier what's fit for a soldier.
Fit, fit, fit for a soldier . . .

First mind you steer clear o' the grog-sellers' huts,
For they sell you Fixed Bay'nets that rots out your guts --
Ay, drink that 'ud eat the live steel from your butts --
An' it's bad for the young British soldier.
Bad, bad, bad for the soldier . . .

When the cholera comes -- as it will past a doubt --
Keep out of the wet and don't go on the shout,
For the sickness gets in as the liquor dies out,
An' it crumples the young British soldier.
Crum-, crum-, crumples the soldier . . .

But the worst o' your foes is the sun over'ead:
You must wear your 'elmet for all that is said:
If 'e finds you uncovered 'e'll knock you down dead,
An' you'll die like a fool of a soldier.
Fool, fool, fool of a soldier . . .

* * *

If you're cast for fatigue by a sergeant unkind,
Don't grouse like a woman nor crack on nor blind;
Be handy and civil, and then you will find
That it's beer for the young British soldier.
Beer, beer, beer for the soldier . . .

Now, if you must marry, take care she is old --
A troop-sergeant's widow's the nicest I'm told,
For beauty won't help if your rations is cold,
Nor love ain't enough for a soldier.
'Nough, 'nough, 'nough for a soldier . . .

If the wife should go wrong with a comrade, be loath
To shoot when you catch 'em -- you'll swing, on my oath! --
Make 'im take 'er and keep 'er: that's Hell for them both,
An' you're shut o' the curse of a soldier.
Curse, curse, curse of a soldier . . .

When first under fire an' you're wishful to duck,
Don't look nor take 'eed at the man that is struck,
Be thankful you're livin', and trust to your luck
And march to your front like a soldier.
Front, front, front like a soldier . . .

When 'arf of your bullets fly wide in the ditch,
Don't call your Martini a cross-eyed old bitch;
She's human as you are -- you treat her as sich,
An' she'll fight for the young British soldier.
Fight, fight, fight for the soldier . . .

When shakin' their bustles like ladies so fine,
The guns o' the enemy wheel into line,
Shoot low at the limbers an' don't mind the shine,

For noise never startles the soldier.
Start-, start-, startles the soldier . . .

If your officer's dead and the sergeants look white,
Remember it's ruin to run from a fight:
So take open order, lie down, and sit tight,
And wait for supports like a soldier.
Wait, wait, wait like a soldier . . .

When you're wounded and left on Afghanistan's plains,
And the women come out to cut up what remains,
Jest roll to your rifle and blow out your brains
An' go to your Gawd like a soldier.
Go, go, go like a soldier,
Go, go, go like a soldier,
Go, go, go like a soldier,
So-oldier of the Queen!

To Wolcott Balestier

Beyond the path of the outmost sun through utter darkness hurled --
Further than ever comet flared or vagrant star-dust swirled --
Live such as fought and sailed and ruled and loved and made our world.

They are purged of pride because they died, they know the worth of their bays,
They sit at wine with the Maidens Nine and the Gods of the Elder Days,
It is their will to serve or be still as fitteth our Father's praise.

'Tis theirs to sweep through the ringing deep where Azrael's outposts are,
Or buffet a path through the Pit's red wrath when God goes out to war,
Or hang with the reckless Seraphim on the rein of a red-maned star.

They take their mirth in the joy of the Earth --
they dare not grieve for her pain --
They know of toil and the end of toil, they know God's law is plain,
So they whistle the Devil to make them sport who know that Sin is vain.

And ofttimes cometh our wise Lord God, master of every trade,
And tells them tales of His daily toil, of Edens newly made;
And they rise to their feet as He passes by, gentlemen unafraid.

To these who are cleansed of base Desire, Sorrow and Lust and Shame --
Gods for they knew the hearts of men, men for they stooped to Fame,
Borne on the breath that men call Death, my brother's spirit came.

He scarce had need to doff his pride or slough the dross of Earth --
E'en as he trod that day to God so walked he from his birth,
In simpleness and gentleness and honour and clean mirth.

* * *

So cup to lip in fellowship they gave him welcome high
And made him place at the banquet board -- the Strong Men ranged thereby,
Who had done his work and held his peace and had no fear to die.

Beyond the loom of the last lone star, through open darkness hurled,
Further than rebel comet dared or hiving star-swarm swirled,
Sits he with those that praise our God for that they served His world.

Tommy

I went into a public-'ouse to get a pint o' beer,
The publican 'e up an' sez, "We serve no red-coats here."
The girls be'ind the bar they laughed an' giggled fit to die,
I outs into the street again an' to myself sez I:
O it's Tommy this, an' Tommy that, an' "Tommy, go away";
But it's "Thank you, Mister Atkins", when the band begins to play,
The band begins to play, my boys, the band begins to play,
O it's "Thank you, Mister Atkins", when the band begins to play.

I went into a theatre as sober as could be,
They gave a drunk civilian room, but 'adn't none for me;
They sent me to the gallery or round the music-'alls,
But when it comes to fightin', Lord! they'll shove me in the stalls!
For it's Tommy this, an' Tommy that, an' "Tommy, wait outside";
But it's "Special train for Atkins" when the trooper's on the tide,
The troopship's on the tide, my boys, the troopship's on the tide,
O it's "Special train for Atkins" when the trooper's on the tide.

Yes, makin' mock o' uniforms that guard you while you sleep
Is cheaper than them uniforms, an' they're starvation cheap;
An' hustlin' drunken soldiers when they're goin' large a bit
Is five times better business than paradin' in full kit.
Then it's Tommy this, an' Tommy that, an' "Tommy, 'ow's yer soul?"
But it's "Thin red line of 'eroes" when the drums begin to roll,
The drums begin to roll, my boys, the drums begin to roll,
O it's "Thin red line of 'eroes" when the drums begin to roll.

We aren't no thin red 'eroes, nor we aren't no blackguards too,
But single men in barricks, most remarkable like you;
An' if sometimes our conduck isn't all your fancy paints,
Why, single men in barricks don't grow into plaster saints;
While it's Tommy this, an' Tommy that, an' "Tommy, fall be'ind",

But it's "Please to walk in front, sir", when there's trouble in the wind,
There's trouble in the wind, my boys, there's trouble in the wind,
O it's "Please to walk in front, sir", when there's trouble in the wind.

You talk o' better food for us, an' schools, an' fires, an' all:
We'll wait for extry rations if you treat us rational.
Don't mess about the cook-room slops, but prove it to our face
The Widow's Uniform is not the soldier-man's disgrace.
For it's Tommy this, an' Tommy that, an' "Chuck him out, the brute!"
But it's "Saviour of 'is country" when the guns begin to shoot;
An' it's Tommy this, an' Tommy that, an' anything you please;
An' Tommy ain't a bloomin' fool -- you bet that Tommy sees!

When Earth's Last Picture Is Painted

When Earth's last picture is painted
And the tubes are twisted and dried
When the oldest colors have faded
And the youngest critic has died
We shall rest, and faith, we shall need it
Lie down for an aeon or two
'Till the Master of all good workmen
Shall put us to work anew
And those that were good shall be happy
They'll sit in a golden chair
They'll splash at a ten league canvas
With brushes of comet's hair
They'll find real saints to draw from
Magdalene, Peter, and Paul
They'll work for an age at a sitting
And never be tired at all.
And only the Master shall praise us.
And only the Master shall blame.
And no one will work for the money.
No one will work for the fame.
But each for the joy of the working,
And each, in his separate star,
Will draw the thing as he sees it.
For the God of things as they are!

THE POEMS OF RUDYARD KIPLING

Available on Amazon

Made in the USA
Coppell, TX
13 June 2021